DANCE

DANCE

POEMS

Lightsey Darst

COFFEE HOUSE PRESS
2013

COPYRIGHT © 2013 by Lightsey Darst
COVER AND BOOK DESIGN by Linda Koutsky
AUTHOR PHOTOGRAPH © Jeffrey Skemp

COFFEE HOUSE PRESS books are available to the trade through our primary distributor, Consortium Book Sales & Distribution, cbsd.com or (800) 283-3572. For personal orders, catalogs, or other information, write to: info@coffeehousepress.org.

Coffee House Press is a nonprofit literary publishing house. Support from private foundations, corporate giving programs, government programs, and generous individuals helps make the publication of our books possible. We gratefully acknowledge their support in detail in the back of this book. To you and our many readers around the world, we send our thanks for your continuing support.

LIBRARY OF CONGRESS CIP INFORMATION
Darst, Lightsey.
[Poems. Selections]
DANCE : poetry / by Lightsey Darst.
pages ; cm.
ISBN 978-1-56689-334-3 (PBK.)
I. Title.
PS3604.A79D36 2013
811'.6—DC23
2013003667

PRINTED IN THE U.S.A.
FIRST EDITION | FIRST PRINTING

LOVE

TREASURE

(hell)

At times it seems to me, said de Jong, as if all works of art were coated with a sugar glaze or indeed made completely of sugar, like the model of the battle of Esztergom created by a confectioner to the Viennese court, which Empress Maria Theresia, so it is said, devoured in one of her recurrent bouts of melancholy.

—*The Rings of Saturn,* by W. G. Sebald,
    translated by Michael Hulse

Treasure

A beautiful house is built with no foundation: so raze the palace to build a prison. Lace
wolves wrap coolly round a girl's loins, their glassed eyes set in lids of fresh onyx.

All last season, the skeletons rose and fell on biers of pack ice—I mean the frames of slaves,
gilt & cast out, amber veins sprayed in a soft net, generous as fish scales in a river's harvest.

Meanwhile, our vacant mansions stand in fields of mud, their windows maze cracked under the strain
of bending idle lines of sight while a single horse, tired of providing scale, rears

& runs: all that was made fine dies in dust; but maids sweep your view lacquered and clean.
No diminution. With two virgin eyes you can see to the raveling edge of this event horizon.

The Ash Palaces. ↓

At her funeral, the princess arias

I love that maybe it's true—swelling in the secret parts, cats killed en masse.
Mercy, how these derelict signs attach, slick allure of this ink even when [poor princess] all flesh

of truth is lost. (They crowd back now in thin-armed millions.) Little trinket of my circlet,
vitrined after my decease, and the Byzantine emperor lost his son, that was weeping, yet

sweet, so lovely in your suit of red velvet, buried my five children with my own tears,
five corsets woven with gold inlay of stars, crescents, and diamonds, spun glass hemispheres,

all going one way, namely, crossing to death. "I love that maybe—anonymous grave, moan
barely cold before my quick burial by the roadside, shall not be found, wax face & hands

fold in a pattern of mere grief, fright & surprise" while so many die all believe it is the scent
of the world. Love me? down to the very gene, viral sheen of my crown & breath spent,

heart gnawn, you see, I didn't make it. [many dismal objects] [Coffined] Can't shake
this mood, this sorrow, not an accurate word. This sense of thin ice & break. Listen:

"Once they'd reached this point, some sort of reckoning was inevitable." "Morbid."
"In nearly all cases, the methods employed against the plague aided its onward spread."

[With quick sighs, as through a veil.]

West General Mourning Warehouse

Start with mirrors of polished metal buried with our dead. Then, among mummies,
some real, some poor, some sham, a price, a several-layered relic, "I dragged my costless soul

into slums of industrial cities "impressively shattering" paint us over in black & gold for a
queen's funeral / a feathered hearse & horses / a "time does change small wounds"—sh:

bereaved customers. "Mother bought my summer gown, fine apple-green cashmere;
I waltzed, but today it's sent to the dyers to be sunk black—such an unlucky shade"

she said, & sighed "not needless things upon our coffin" (mourning in all its branches, made
of scrap metal, these hours happen, and no varnished heartwood is enough to hold

your body, nude, with its skin & dress of ice & snow (sick, but rivers of jasmine run
your haunches, flanks, balls of perfume in your plaits, melting over dinner's tallow while richest

pearls loop across her bodice. The highest luster (besides those who died in fields,
secret places) for a kingdom's jail, cold & choiceless, on the occasion of the first human

auction—able to shape metal or carve stone—alluvial electrum, embossing, repoussé,
we knit our queen's encrusted & gilt neckpiece, a belt & garter, ring on each finger,

stylized chrome flowers, headband of bronze leaves, & sixty attendants in pectoral ornaments.
Lay as a fringe then fell as a cascade . . . lattice, the dead were / deceased wore beryl,

lapis lazuli, carnelian & agate (splendidly adorned)—rosettes set, hair bound
in polychrome inlay rings, gold gazelle heads, slaves & sapphires probably from Sri Lanka . . .

White sapphire white plague

When I did walk, I saw always a great many poor wanderers at a distance. Adieu to this
hysteria zoo so late twentieth-century gunpowder amulet "don't mind if I do" new bijoux bright

as fever eyes. Your poor people walked the streets until they fell down dead,
fragrant with violet or heliotrope" perfumed graves for the demimonde; enter this prison,

with several straight, broad staircases, insect eyes at interstice" & each minister listens in
"angel with a sword—we hear" here forever but feel each carcass, ruby crossed, glassed

out. "In those days, ropes of ermine, smotherings of bone silk, queen in red corsets beautiful
without her head" so we listen, "house locked up, sealed on a scream of a jade design"

the nothings. "A home shut up, a man cries inside, his maiden daughters say good-bye
without turning their heads." necessary to deceive the dead a little | & darling if I'd known

I'd never have come, but blood remains our most precious metal . . . burning glass. Then
all people so embroidered by desire, all people, the best people, caught in their houses

surprised, an outward sign of a defect of the soul suddenly sprouted at the groin, prone
& helpless while others board up your doors outside. A whole family gone,

a world of opulence here—clear velvet teardrop (cuts across the shoulderbone)
(hacks through the marrow) arrow "women will seduce men with them" & sharp stone

blue frost fox bolero, diamond & rubber ("does not need") torque strikes starved eyes
lined in black & streaking eyeless rim of soot does not want" immediate plexiglass [pity of

your gross wound] with green kid gloves, and you know the story.—Everything
managed with such care. As for the poor man, whether he lived or died, I don't remember.

Cleveland

Last seen wearing a yellow blouse, gray tweed skirt, white bobby socks & black-bow
ballerina flats. a bracelet-length sleeve is simply more elegant, but no tourniquet is enough

& corrodes the flesh beneath. [go home girls] Black velvet rich on both her sides
(speak each way) corrupts, & rend apart the tacked-down tears to hope, enchain & out glides

[sorry love] "tucked up today's scar" ruched blood in a narrative "so fast lord loud &
at the same time (as in ashes they find your gold more easily / beautiful" hand

(beautiful") that ambles, spiderlike, through her unguent pots in search . . . you swallow
enigmatic jewel, twelve emblems & a secret motto" / the story's gore—eternity or so

in malachite & kohl. Those pleasing girls, out late, looking glass guardrail and I walked
into my own—it was cold there—thus the furs. Smooth walls" so thin hands take

back each necklace of poisoned hearts—how once hung, she thinks / nothing /
nothing" torture. birchbark skin signed in bruise" nothing thrown in thrown back, nothing

created in the minds of people" & pieces of bone have been found engraved
"nothing is completely certain" "quiet please" lace-crucifix inlay & from a bleak cave

exile a certain lawless being to the limit of it (I) (you) (sister) was a fracture in amethyst
jet tunic with pompadour skirt, braided crystal necklace, studded stilettos, we wear flame-kissed

cowl-neck evening dresses to the funeral, in a froth of romantic seafoam ruffles
The much-respected queen mourned for the remaining forty years of her life."

[*Muted with the hand. Deeper now.*
Keep an undervoice ready to go on
when the lead falters.]

Hunchback

I was painted, always in black" [dust years] "with bars of narrow dark love-ribbon" / we
bury like dogs, resurrectionless. As signs of sorrow forsake. [love] soot, edged with ermine

(mink to ink) flame satin & knife-edged falling collars [we fail]. Forsake silk—
wearing instead homespun, a new mourning. Scarlet to mourn, dun to bury, ivory

to rejoice—crotch like a gorgeous cave—in rooms hung with yards of sloe cloth [sex]
death tapestries, lovely / "I saw such falls" / dull damask hangings, arras & dermis

pierced with gold, socketed, jawbone gilt & humerus to the hilt, hip topped
& clavicle coated, slicked in [justice] [pleasure] [Pleiades] not steel, it bites / bleed

white at the funeral of a child. Velvet cry. Often they were destroyed—stars
are permanent, worth staring: "bury me below winter" since sixty years of grisaille

& crimson to my execution" only dull smoke silk & crepe. Only a blank
hereafter, shut sky, "please seek an antidote"—note the black undersleeves: she wore it

after the death of her twelve-year-old son with a sable hurt, silver net &
dagger headdress trimmed with dull jet & gold / to the fire, the exhumation,

her coronation—daintily this / "white-trimmed parasol above my head" passion
for fashionable mourning dress flourishes undimmed among what signs "and now

covet skins & brocades" she wore it, and asked, what loss? earth to earth & I feel
a mineral longing myself. Diamonds are blind & gold is cold, but topaz / always believe

in decaying wards thousands a family & its cousins coughing, lungs fray so
Upperclass women were never without it / they never reverted to white ones again.

The Ash Palaces. ↑

Shield

Once a duke bought a vase—sent for it in his scrawl in oak-gall ink on virgin skin.
"No expense to be spared," he wrote, and three centuries on, you see the result. Here

the flowing river, blue enamel spiral fruitful with fishtails & scales, and the velvet keel
(razoring) of the pleasure boat the duchess sailed on her wedding day, beaten

gold is the deck & silk the water it runs on, oars of nightingale feathers that sing a seventh
paradise ground to a paste & tossed in the cup for a favorite's sweetest sip of arsenic—

agate inlay the eyes of the eunuchs who row to a rib-bone's beat, pearl the teeth of the girls
who fan her with new-woven nebulae, & here a captive bee in amber, mid-diadem, purrs & whirrs

its wings of violet net, its sting self-curved & soft to the touch: touch, & taste: perpetual
honey wells from a secret spring.—The opium poppies once dreamed, but their smoke is spent.

Here, a trio of dancers on fresh grass smile. The beryl they stand on is sharp & brittle, so
when they step too hard, it shards & so you see these drops of garnet, here & here, & how

this one winces as she turns? The worry in their eyes, observe, is opal—it shifts & silver bells
render their cries. Too, a scar on a slave's face is abalone, glossy cicatrix

that opens under the topaz lash to show lavish carnelian lips you'd like to kiss—
clockwork, like this execution scene with still-breathing corpse & hidden door that slides

open over a ruby knot of heart, its beat stilling to silence as you watch.
—He forgot, while a village raked its fields for jasper. At last the message: yes, your wish—

and finished, this great urn sat in an alcove, angled so its glazed lid's mauve fruit & tongue
hint the master, last nude that hides behind a curtain woven with greedy saints

(hanged—sisters, griffons, pink-floret-smell of painted silk, no blood on gold leaf reaper's
scythe, those dainty pumps, high-heeled with carmine bows and fresh-cut flowers—viral sin

& tear, the latest in designer tulips). Viewer, measure her curved confine, you'll find a mess of
dead men can be packed, rib to neck, inside. And not a crack—was never moved

& these luxuries

                                            unicorn foal ornamental fur"
                                  on a champagne-suede bustier with
                            in transparent wolf-pelt teardrop
                        ostrich, stripped sternum draped
Brushing her bruise eyes. wails kohl & lids of steel. laves flesh in gold dust. moth-eaten
face of our mistress rarely seen as she dances amid fine things, wasting, stroking with satin fingertips—
                    like Cleopatra, she bathes in lynx brains & swans' blood,
                        crocodile glands & pulverized coral, brick, civet, ambergris
                          & mink, confections of mercury, hogs' bones, all creatures
                            we must raid, pervert in order to
                                persist, perfume" at any cost as this lust
                                      shakes us into

astrakhan w/ panne velvet train guipure lace w/ broadtail pearl-painted silk chemise
w/ infant nail paillettes so pay, take a broke limb, drape it, artful slashes as if you made

love in a rose thicket. Once all was clean, now "darling, I hide nothing" creeps through our city like dye
in a vein" "don't breathe on me" collar of emerald on a jade-eyed captive corrupts, once "I was worth more

than an alley of museums, now "sent away all of value on the last horse cart. bodies. bodies.
seen so much I bleed at the eyes, my love. go away from here. not safe" a smashed cathedral glass, a

slick black animal skin. The plague in black lacquer. Plague in green pleather, plague
in zircon-encrusted sockets, ultimate bling, ultimate slaughter, baby. Ruby to body

as worldly goods to blood, still nude to fresh kill as platinum hilt to drive-by—garnet
is a poor substitute. You are a poor substitute. Mink is to ink as cash to ash—burn,

& buy me a cobalt miniskirt short enough to catch a chill
—always cleared away by morning.

"When you say handiwork, picture

we two in our white dresses that day before, under the vine & side by side stitching
baby clothes for our new brother. That peace—Father in the sunlight looking on / picture

me with my thimble, Sister, slashed as a sleeve is, thorn-prickt, woundful, pounced with so fine scars
the stars   / whose arm or bone or scrim of flesh

To trim a lace." Trinket. needle—right through my wrist" glass clear
& tiny like a pin's madness—but you will learn this trade, you will

stitch to itch as kill to ill, wealth to health as cloak to lock, a cash flare
in each fear—just so a vacant palace faces a vacant palace over barren land or air, nightmare
                                              is to gold as cancer to glister, now
                                        all things glisten, listen in on this
atom: you're dull the way you are. Hock your parents' ashes for a
spot of black taffeta—shaped like a coach-&-four—or red, cut from Spanish leather" sword

/ Examiners, Searchers, Cutters, Nurses, Watchmen, Keepers, Burners, Buriers
slaughter is to laughter as skin to kin. But [Sister] this most grievous story must be told . . . seeing

they are all dead & are to be huddled together into the common
bath of coal, May dew & lambs' caul / rotten oak ash / blind as a land mine

cut in heavy satin silk with empty bodice draped in dove-gray chiffon (indeed
it was very dreadful) & in demand now are bombproof tombs.

                                        nipples] & hang, gnaw
                                    molten lead [gild your
Helpless among all I lost" very suddenly, truly, with a view through an arch toward a bridge over
away, help me see: great span of the fresco lost—were there fields? (is an oil slick, nuclear spill, detonation

& it came upon them like an armed man [women will destroy men with them], this
extreme hourglass whittled from flesh & grave wax . . . "Queen's famous wardrobe" . . .
                                    does not speak to us, as it were—only answers

"I feel nothing / nothing / but pretty hair bracelets, or other (empty,
but in profound affliction) jewelry cut from fragments of exploded shells

& continue these observations without doors."

Spectacle   & crepe |
broadcloth, coal silk
sorrow. only dull black
Lusterless, it flares out. "This sapphire bestows blessings on the wearer"
burr eyes, burnt through, all suede trim & fur feathers too sick to dance dancing

draught of hemlock. "quivers going down. we have no right, stealing
this precious air. we glide windblown only when you sleep then we swarm," high & my
"angels gnawing an animal body"—
titanium canine, the flesh never wise, eyes
"like blue glass against" "all that falls" [your mouth—gore pink—little filed teeth
said [all prettiness cut by] "that form [your pretty knife] feels deliciously
eaten away" so slip
in coffin / corset / iron maiden,
listeners level to your whip-
stitch lips a poppy slash . . . "By degrees, his head sunk into his body, until at last his face
could no more be seen, and shortly thereafter he died." Pity of fracture, pity of life. Seen
clear through, girls coo
over clavicles hovering light broke ("penetrated") ("perforated") our
hurtness. What acids
bird of paradise shining in her spun-glass hair, steel artery
as a passion was I ever lovely architrave, breastbone sheath" thus the empress gathers her own quills. half a
injured in the fray. / & cast off, cut down / charm against evil / baby, charm yourself with pink
sequin shifts, fine hands crawl & graze, each year
as if you'd never been there, angel of death
or smoothed limbs, salt-buffed
eyeless
centerless fire eye. applause as the teeth undo you

*[Plaintively, allowing the hair
to fall from your head.]*

The invention of torture

        —White lead poisoning for all these apertures onto perfectly drawn shadows.
Fleet stabbings in a perfect garden pierce those roses, steel & what kind of person would"

feathers blood-dipped scatter in dirty snow, these hostile symbols of perfect virtues
& mines lie empty at Golconda. At last. As an arsenal lasts, arrow by arrow (true)

"and in ancient times, how dead space was valued . . ." so dead men were made (inside us
cathedrals) & snowdrifts of glistening fat) seaweed still wrapped around your leg), smiles, "does

my long hair trouble you—ripples like chain mail. I'm a saint. Let me put it up before your
axe"—"stretches forth his shaking hands" ready to know, but the blade antique, diamond-sharp

      cast silver, its panels / nothing needs to understand you" / its scenes
prance, imperial stallion bridled in ropes of knuckles, platinum trappings, marches tossing

blank sightless head. Nor could anybody help another; so I went on past—
      panels of pearls & pearls & precious stones / heart-shaped hurricane, organ of fire

      or go to your own house, if possible, as I mentioned before, & there sit, grow faint,
& die. this kind of dying lines her veins in blue paint, pliant as

*

a swan, cut open & laid flat to make a sign. Finding yourself again in the asylum.
* * * soulful execution of rabbit and gall, whiteness of powdered pigbone

finding yourself again in the train station. No, the dead wood does not need
to embrace you . . . restrained with woven crystal strands (abandoned auditorium)

& tusks of the last African elephant bar what appears to be a door (still).
Walls stand so clearly on the discovery of perspective, yet how they fall

/ oh well: a royal painter butchers several dogs to make the moral image of our loyalty.
Look on with soiled eyes: stunning constructions of straps, skins, & souls" spin
in mirror discs

cracked—diamonds glint
nonetheless. all a fashionable bruise. infected house shut down
for little girls in red leather, lists of the lost printed each week & how dark

this stage where the masquerade has closed. Good-bye, my love—they run so lightly off
& have not held you since, even two bodies make a pile pale in satin ice—see

this broken object rekindle against familiar air: lift the engraving
against the ungraved scene, see it flare / into life

*

So many people tragically ignore (often you feel no pain at all)

Their faces should be hidden and their eyes cast down
Hematite in ashy veins—of gold with pierced—of white satin in bloodstone stains

*
/

—this opening in the columns: several ribs askew, indicative
of flight or fright—and a shadow dogging you "did not see the oncoming") forced, or lovely

neck draped with war-patterned fabric, she turns aside and murmurs,
"what does it matter what I wear. dead anyway. that I am fine is for

/
/

my soul to feel" a train so long she stretches under the hooves of her painted horse, a haze
of artery veil—this lifetime of jewels & precious stones still ahead of us / & gaze of viral fear

"They never thought of me as they fitted the dress to me" face
floating in isolation amid her finery, she sighs,

*
*

& still a kind of crying voice what can you know? This horizon is a thin thing . . . a
child bride's circlet left to tarnish now she falls. —Others, no sign but the mark, thus.

/
/

Quarry

My own flesh. One lustrous eye pried loose by a child's
"Elegant" the duchess cried, then flung her fox fur over. "Whose

reach out, rot, unhinge—corpse poison cureless, whose dream /
city, surrendering burnished gold, gold through the slaughter by

in a wilderness of mass grave. "So fine—my skin in finger pleats,
filigree. so fine I would have wanted one myself" [in the grave is

unless / tested on animals. No help. Recall the damasks you
live under acanthus for accuracy—no one can say the artist won't

to make one gram of dream, field mown & milled, distilled, to
of bone & big-eyed as a Paris model" but you must peer closely

rears your triumph—unharmed entry into the plague city (inside
touch. "They want to see beauty, always, but it doesn't work like

useless] white rabbit is not able. Design of an elegant casket,
ripe belly, parts buried separately & all "my desires carried off,

eater of all whose "sister I was happy to be made clean [discards
rot gold, aura of gore, each finger so ring-heavy each gesture cost

soma embroidered in blood, believe, pearled, Veiled, I spoke only
a cognac back in a leopard throat, one flick ignites a bravura fireball,

vial of flesh or essence of puma masked with sweet cedar or that
eyes a man who buys a virgin flings her on wraps his limb in her

meal, then a pearl, then a palace] small change of a child's spine.
you will always have with you" want not / of such there's millions.

curious nail—coral nectar streams from a socket. Touch it.
limbs—such luxury to be mixed feed for a poppy field, to

want not / wants more: "moved with wonder to plunder our
the heels like living, breathing" [sickening, we root out

spangled scale to a dry gem of gall, scalp peeled & ormolu,
what the market leaves] "gunman / cash / mass" expert in slaughter

stood still for? Those scenes, leaves artfully arranged, each rape
know what it looks like" ripped veil of face. an acre ground

yield a single dye. In this tapestry refugees, a varicolored heap
to see what suffers in her sheer lamé spangle, how each panel

our corset maggots gnaw)—satin smile erodes by time,
that" outcries of the miserable oh misery! not able to bear, as a

but the interred breaks it. draw the dissection of a poor woman's
peeled loose" oil from your backs, gut-strip the veneers you

your bones are darling, ruby excrescences]" Cannot get up under
empire—angel with a sword" I heard wrung each carcass, sore

to the one before me"—glistening, vinyl night, he sighs, tip
poor hovels. But complete, the great ewer cost her less than a

extinct [ask the Princess de Lamballe] godless their gun-oil
sleek skin, drapes her silk against his aging armor. [she wants a

the grasslands have been churned under. "our jewels, arsenic
but I never possessed one of my own [till the blood runs free

Look down: from this perilous vantage you may admire
unfurling dance as the great house crush collapse (workers

Xanadu dancing tonight (festoon of blood diamonds. gunmetal hips. coffins shot
emptiest of ice palaces, I see the murder" my murder, my

bordered with ____, glistening with ____ ("buried my")
lilies grow (daughter. husband. sister. lament

ought to be. green-graves [hold a relic or perfume
only a cut of air" short fever followed by an all-fire—blazing spire, this throne

dream of a great ruin before a vast arc of triumph—once an angels' city, now
Without stars. In narrow chambers at the hearts of pyramids, boldly

tell yourself "it never suffered never knew" but opening, confirm
houses sealed up over the dead [lonely dead] we go on building this

seventy-four-thousand-dollar set of china" whose hands whose sole shake whose
halt tremble, poor man's hands quiver as he begs ("my daughters")

harvest in a valise" tossed in a fire, & every query anesthetized against
velvet burnout, lasered rose (why not a rose of red steel)"

treasure, easily broken into a powder (thousands, he said, sweeping the temple
rash on the face of the earth. [corrosion of unnamed gem

in stone is a prayer no more. [down a flayed throat
heaven lined in animal skins. face built of fragments, as

Elysium piled over the usual boneyard, fed on the usual infant. you'll gut-strip,
listen: "our minefields grow bird sanctuaries"

when he was almost dead, & cried   will I return" / only shudders once. this pile of furs
"I want what I want" at first,   I believe in the next world. & after / brought to the dyer
  sold to strangers. thirst,   starving, sowing a seed of steel in the neck. but this is a celebration
  her lost sister   have come to us cramped, maimed, scarred, [pity] out of the prison house

26

[Lie down in the open space: let fragments
be heaped around you.]

[we hear war is over] a man-made paradise. "your hazy beauty, helpless empty
                    unhurt, lucky men!") through a million of discarded flesh is

silk) (money from cast-off arms) a prisoner scaling a wall looks back. please
            [   ] into etched mute mouths. a body in the light of the lamp

murmurs a wanderer on the saint's road. ruin. lover, in that rank cavity do
            & slaughter the witnesses. We admire this hollow where a yes

"seems to come out of nothing—nothing—then a spar—where before ascends
        ringed with artificial animals that hail you king & finally you, slave,

heap of dust" (mechanical scorpions) but children sleep easier in a home
Say this wilderness of building, say what you like. How will you (knowing the cost)

"corrupted did my architecture proceed in dreams" ash our rich
        roil. rot city. clockwork vultures. some not able to bear, as a gentian

"your pavers heavy heavy on my chest" & such cluttered cataclysm—the lame, the
        for alms, asking / where is the river that ran here? where the sweet farm

hellebore [more war] (poisonous) help me] against the ____, the
        pure air in there, breathless) bear passing pain for sake of] no

never. fell from all parts in striking confusion
hold your worth in my hand" unending. "When the arches fell, a smoke a prayer

emptied by cold. throw their bodies out at windows] all souls. and so
            a gravemound is built. all veneer. and so

ravage into a new pleasure. how spirit jangles when it's naked how [whose arm
            dream. and glimpse, on their restless fronts, stars"

"was so beclouded & crusht. and   we believed it. but what gleams, an idol, stripped
  inside the bones, gems. under the gems, guns   inner war] or against bloodred satin
snapped the veins, let out the black ugly blood, & weeping)   shone in more than your torture
hurt. glittering triple ply across a vast expanse. gorgeous immortal work/   he dropt loose. &

                            he was cured"

No shortage of symbols

Witness this rib cage, complicated in the extreme: here wind surrounds a white pine
casket, white pain) the structure: stop: of a vessel (was in hiding / snow down tracks

this room of a dream's construction. The cost of grand burials grows enormous, with
the death's head upon them, within one month after our departure, improved

into a dull, lifeless blackness. Only a few cents this reckless, for you" no wrist
listens closer in flame in coma the primary no, avalanche it was all (says the text) a mental

disease." It parts, waters of the Red Sea close after, what after there is none. empty. Curtains
end this fine chain of impressions your mind could indeed be represented on paper or in

a nightclub fire. We dig old graves but even the best embalming only ends in corpses.
Always / eternity, the infinite, immensity, of time, space, divinity & tombs / Lawless, this

intertwining of superstructures / as evidence at a show trial, as a pattern of stars,
latterly seen above—because a skeleton was thought necessary—all this we built, because

it is necessary to sweep away the dust of previous palace—upon understanding our
shoulder's musculature | I still hold forth hope of a pure Palladian window arriving in a
dream

"I've been looking forward to another life—the afterlife, I've been calling it"

Strokes her litter of rabbits—a "birth defect," but she marvels at their soft fur,
"and so many / Diana in the tunnel / shining arms wreathed in slave diamond & mink

slapped, kept / a token of truce in the birth, blessed bone cradle & black revolver
bring me a thousand roses painted kohl. I've lost my lover to cocaine" this fashion

for burial by torchlight, so coruscating in chrome beads, roars, lolls "saucer-eyed &
wasp-waisted, your gorgeous corpse" swathed in plum & crimson tulle or crystal-

beaded corset toned down for good taste with the dullness of sick or chiffon
though darling decease's a silk pocket and these devil-ray stilettos all season

but in gray & silver or lilac & gold and so on but not gold & white
why do we kill ourselves—stop me I can't stop myself jewel-bright

enamel & pearl floral necklace, blue satin pumps, frayed-edge blouse"
like cancer lungs. She wore it. X-ray vision gleans no skeleton beneath the show.

        afterlife"

29

floor (to poor) to end
core pays for your marble

Sister, we are cold   rich ripped stitch. Each
before a face to save skin to

Pearl to ilk as silk to sick, slick surface of platinum leg & bone shone to a liquid shield held
& emerald age, an avalanche pauses, advances, thinks, her tinkling jewels chiseled froze framed
in the nicest pose & winter unburdens our
gun fodder of their fur, reveals the work
under their sun-stung skin. diaphanous

"I was fire in several animals, tried, but stayed metal-tongued, pelt slick with gasoline
& slip darkling darling beaded in arrows & steel traps. several daggers chandeliered to those
ears, a prick's a mere
sore's a canker

structure [suture] of justice. the exchange—one who dies & one who lives, etc.—
is building for us all, is sorting up several symmetrical entrances to the illness, bridge
overwhelmed, sea overwhelmed, windows open on

passing through the carnival. "I spend my twenties gazing in store windows" "pearls big as knuckles"
[incidental violence] can be frozen for hundreds of years this way—

this pale stone & crystal fortification. (slash is to lash to ash, & sh: as ice unbreakable
/

/

so doth the dust destroy the diamond.

A few flaws were thought nothing. Mountain of light, cut down
to a dim steel overpass in a dingy city, "stone
of an inferior water" the images

["In your glorious metropolis—a Saturday—we disappeared. Darling I hide nothing"
break up in surf. hurt form aches, a bent arabesque, open-to-the-snow eye. spatter, dried, signs your
message—cancerous

garden seeded with gems so nothing grows but a thin bare grass that clings
to the dirty faces of spare sapphires. but all prisons. / but not all
rooms are prisons. but
all windows

diseased, beloved, or never there (plait like a horsetail) (in a drawer) (got burnt up in a house fire)
(flame-red embraces) & all you have left: arm of a barred spiral galaxy
whips out past you in a spasm an
epilepsy of yes.

Several miles of prison, up / Several fragments in search of a
& outward (not the same cruelty) (not the same mercy) centering gut / entrail / to be from /
<mobile reliquary
head in a jar, all sudden violence, the rib cage that receives. There tumble forth rubies /

---

† After the palace is ransacked we retreat to inner quarters. Courts of rot. On a silver plate, hate; in a cut crystal, bile; on a silk tapestry, auto-da-fé. Flax hanks of her hair; fragment of a brainpan, filigree;

cloisonné cache of guns. In the bank, canker crawling across mounds of cash one cent one shot "All lost" worth more than people, many people can be plowed under, repeat crash, mess suicide, slide a trapped tidal

† surge, wave's urge in a box you tip to watch the tiny village scatter, scream "a system is better for a few well-planned shocks a system

---

† Typically the product you purchase lives in the back of a locked removal van. Typically nothing (between dresses) of lasting interest." In the no one rooms, wheat wasn't what fed us. Witness this

† triumph of the skinning art . . . everything is dangerous. You'd want it too: milk mixed with silver ore, for imagine: now your fate is several hundred miles wide and extends across both oceans"

---

† Feel your lapel to know the content of your soul. Feel your wool. None shall wear any
cloth of gold, tissue, nor fur of sables, except duchesses, marquises, with gold, silver, or pearl, saving

countesses, partlets, sleeves [Listen: no air to speak of] velvet in crimson, carnation; furs—black genets, lucerns; none shall wear any [in a cameo frozen like an ancestor. resist] velvet gowns, fur of leopards, embroidery of silk, & trimmed with pearl; none satin, damask, or tufted taffeta in [vanishing] shall not cloth of gold or silver, tinseled satin, silk, or cloth mixed & embroidered; none shall wear

skin of the boy in the photo, $3,500 to hold—"always wanted, never had one of my own"

*   *

Greyhound. Sleek, strong, but a meaningless life.
600. Will do everything perfect.

Graphite

I built it first as a shelter. This was before
I built this maze as a hospital. Arrayed the cells

You could see a long way—skylights,
I built it first as asylum. I built it

You see these slums. I designed them—years
pleasure, now hovels—I built it not

morgue, no, a glasshouse, a prison all eyes
                            will see no
cut out, a kidney, heartstone—offers me
five thousand for the boy but what could I

this plague began in a hush, it began on a heave
I tried, but too strong—that fire or flood, I forget,

fight, so I saw, as on an island, cut off
so I sold or lost the house they'll come back to

obscured by a jade screen—we don't recognize
moss-green, she smiles upon us for a last

You can buy a child. You can buy
                            this one
I see far off such light—light of the great
conflagration—all the infected & their state,
it's cursed we will not go on. We must go on
the first city, filled with dead, must be
heaps of ashes" my life's been ruined" and I
down like a curtain. Certain pleasure awaits,

sleek head a stroke
no visible wound. perhaps the perfume overcame"

gathered around me as a garment every stitch
And thus I built.

the war. I built it to house their markless bodies,
for light & air, walled orchard, flowers,

*

atria, miles of glass—gone now, bricked in
not as a prison but a pesthouse—no

ago, for the queen, but ill, she forgets. Once
as a slaughterhouse but a garden—no

terror like the present. Softly, the war

was very simple but very happy. My life
after all I have other children. I built

*

of wind. it rose up on an inward tide;
its fingers stripping my fingers—could not

*

can't reach, so left, & now, no remedy for never,
if they come back, they never will now—
                            cut off by a bank of rose,
the trace effaced, her familiar eyes no more
once, we wince from her sheen. But this is past

*

& wandering among the palaces (vacant by now)

burnt; how many families fleeing the smoke
they cry. All the ground raked up,
abandoned. There I saw what remains. Only
will wander to the world's end
a measure of molten gold a hold on each

"I know my haven is upon me"

*

"I know my heaven is upon me" still

*

I built it. Your absence was the keystone

[*In counterpoint. Walk through the available
space, pleading, calling to no one.*] →

all plant matter, innocent"

                  artifact in order to realize its ending
*   grows eyes"

Penetrable landscape, arranged
art horror. love to touch, stroke,   smothers like so many in my family. I've seen
                      broken, pretty shatters"
*   *

when through a desolate wasteland I   heavy under heavy: fractures
        brought the marble for the monument—
Vaultless. this   hung over us night & day & into
sleeps a turmoil, perpetual.   You are   *
                *

the oh madness. tore her hair   * & now
all that can be is seen.   Uncover   the heavy brain, so that
         the bare heart, unravel

all that is seen is all that can be.   You too are carbon, stilling
Titanium lasts. The bearer fades,   empty until filled, free until taken
        Thousands have no language. have no
[netted organ—seven pairs of needles]   —More war, less fear to feel it in,
                *   *

[but all this time   grows in the dark,
the city below the city   mutant fields of steel flowers—]   * please say not so many, no
*

Strike at the silence as if to ring

         it—vanishes   each afternoon achieves . . .
                    But I keep

what I can" desolation. the depth   *
of this keeps getting deeper,   "and all that I saw, I claimed for
         the kingdom"   don't you know me, behind my
& yours] a prison rises   facial design"

along each embrace   in the service of light [she gleams
        This is a delicate procedure. So listen
but we've kept nothing (sores.   poisons rust corsage this formless
quarry of enormous shattering losses"   names of workers blurred

digging under digging) thousand   landmines, sleeps, carved eye buttons that see

. . . trapped flowers in these inks   does not matter panes are broken . . . . . . bruised with erasure
        several hundred thousand miles of
                     *

*
dust"   still, darling, Nothing
is destroyed, only alters.   alters"

Beauvais

      "I a maker of beautiful hulls" transform
this multitude of useless bells |

"torrent of stones. the cracks are moving"

["paradise, erased in a few hours"]
["god's bones,

                   Vision of a pristine skeleton.
                   Vision of hell—

["And it was marvelous, though sad, to behold"]

      (spend our lives in
shadows of unfinished)

Beauvais

Our cathedral climbed higher than any in France before it fell.

Waking after nightmare, you hear
light feet worrying your stairs. The masons whisper

something about the vault,
a buttress too filigreed, does not support. Workmen crushed.

The rustling feet scud from front door to stair,
then climb up. Someone, no one there.

What the sun set on, did not rise. Priests cried.
We feared we would not understand each other, Babel

broken out in our town. You go back to sleep and never
hear those steps again. Ghost at the edge of knowing,

what undid you: that last outward turn—
shattered walls of spinel. We were told

we were unwise, but we'd built so high
by then we had to go on. Bury them there.

Now, an aerial photo shows the height we never touched.

Burning library

Life was regarded as ended, wearing large gem-set earrings.
I am speaking now of people made desperate . . . black onyx.

I have been a thief, I have been an adulterer, I have been a murderer.
Each rung an arm, jade eyehole, platinum-lapped bone. You hid your rhinestones

in skull boxes: "buried my wife" a public desolation of elderberry stain, drawn
with carved ivory index fingers. Belladonna for your / la belle vie / kicks skirts, shows

those they call the buriers, at other times bearers. An Universal Charm: but what
is that to you? Stop the dead-cart."

Taken in after-
glow: skin licked to a woundless / blue contralto. & eyes / like a warning, warming /
                                                                    frozen river

ZODIAC

(earth)

Instructions:
To find your horoscope, draw a card from an ordinary deck. Discard diamonds or clubs.

Stillwater

Then we walked down to the river and noticed the bridge
carved up into compliant sections, one pushed south: no passage.

Disassembled—or to dissemble, as in an eighteenth-century novel, to set aside
notions of truth and embroider false leaves below falser flowers. Having lied,

then the near present opens at seams, we can change our lives
as we've always been asked to, yes so the tower crumbles but what saves

us will unfurl lotus-like in the center of this, I promise. In Grand Central I watched a man
& woman kiss—but was he reading news above her shoulder? Span

of her embrace over sports scores, his eyes divide along an inside line, private life
betrays any promise. I was so tired then. And I will always love you. Since the light

is dim, what can you see of me but turning limbs. The heart, for certain,
remains hidden—I'm sorry. But we didn't even want to cross the river then,

we were busy in antique stores telling stories, walking in old rooms
with all their secret drawers empty but priced high, as if something still were in them.

Dreamliner still on schedule, Boeing says
Nectromancy. The perception of the inner nature of things.

"My chains"

I did not run off, but I walked off, believing that to be all right.
A speeding ball of fire was seen over north Florida and southern parts of Georgia

yesterday, reported by a mother–daughter pair driving west in a blue wagon.
"Eyes piercing the upper air like one in a dream"

—that's Sojourner, a free woman, but equally true for this apparition, mother
and daughter agree. And it had a tail—this in bright afternoon—neither

superstitious, both scientific, they fear no ends yet
reject all explanations. It was not ___, it was not ___. The mother paints

a still life with field & comet, leaving out for simplicity any human sign, that sign
for peaches in the middle distance, one man bending over a dry stalk in a field,

any buried history or groan from some escaping past. The daughter approves, &
so it is rendered, permanent. They didn't name it. They watched it leave them in the sky.

*Man with blood on his hands charged in Minneapolis stabbing
Dance. A feeling of joy about life coming to the surface.*

Shunt

"He who does not dance does not know the world."
With a verified burglar alarm you're busting out the side of your purple heart when

silver monolith of clear pain, unrelenting, unforeseen
today is dangerous. Driving on the underpass a disaster near as

"When it cleared I saw big girders sticking out of the river at odd angles yes,
just send everything, everything you've got, it's terrible,

it's what happens. You want someone to understand you
("still here") so you laugh or scream / "what is the world coming to

its vacant eyes its staring holes" / Still, sidewalks, "I love you too" hawkweed
not yet flowering in the median, roots wrecking the road, tomorrow's May Day & a fat

legally blind man topples along for all to see, he hums to himself crossing north
while his bus breathes LOVE across its ass & five seconds slip polished by like apple seeds.

Police: home intruder kisses sleeping woman
Ecstasy. Addicted to drugs.

Recognize me

You must help others channel their emotional turmoil into something positive, for
a star "is more than a verbal structure or series of such structures," understood

nothing of the text that tears a speaker's legs below the fold, he appears for
four instants severed. Understand almost nothing, poor moan, helpless

"seems we live in an era of disasters" series of structures, i.e., a city, un-
locked, the people having left in fear of a cyclone / invading army / avalanche—

strange, though; it does seem to be direr here than before, a perspective Dürer
would carve out grunting "pale horse, pale rider, riderless horse" is a horse

a symbol or substance, a city's highest spire, though all children like signs your own
destruction will never seem a sign to you. More than a series

of herbal structures, i.e., a field gone gold
with summer's long wait, horsemint and slash pine & rising but

now it's gone, the neuron that linked, held / a childhood neighborhood / permanently
shuttered the structure "is more than a map of your mind's meaningless sunderings /
                                                                              sparkings"

"Spare part heart" beats in lab
Oryctomancy. By means of excavated objects.

Asphyxia

Decode this, she said, meaning fuck you big daddy.
Less interesting, less informed. We are more informed, of course it was all a dream

(food, corn, gas) but it's my dream, that means I matter, & where's
the death in all this? Flatliner. I just don't know. Too much writing. There is a clutter

obscuring meaning, the clutter is the meaning, as in "a task of interpretation has been"
encrusted with "disorientation after spending time alone" . . . parents should watch out for

the unexplained universe. It was "one last breath," clear enough
for you? You love life marked, no contradictions, "find a pure light" too much

like a prison system. I'm looking for truth. It grovels, it's slimy, all the same I'm
in search of "one definite and simple line of understanding" / fainting game.

Police: man had sex with picnic table
Dust. Concealing questionable activities.

Out, out

Don't you recognize me? Watch the flicker until it trickles, heart's river running
dry—why, shame about your legs, sir, I think I read them on the nightly news, blown

off in a car bomb, correct? was it Kabul or that hellhole my sister calls it, hasn't been
but she does cashier at Mills Fleet Farm out on 94 near Madison well who better with

all those *Newsreeks* she reads between blizzards. One day she leans in, whispers
(frowning face) "whether to die, in any way, feels a moment of choice? the blood

bending to—at what point in the burning will a soul say it's enough, a last breath—
and when [Nicorette sir, sure] can we shut our concern like a messenger's case, they

died instantly—at that moment no more suffering passed the walls of the body, tell me
[Guns-n-ammo] when they kicked him the corpse jerked merely reflexively, the soul

from the gasoline onward felt nothing—off-camera, they used anesthetic" [yes sir] she hurt
for the flesh, it haunted her. And this is what news is: a machine to transfer pain. Never

the less, she gardens: stargazer lilies. And one day she said to me, Amazing
how pink they are. You'd think that color stolen. But from what. Nothing living"—

Lionheart

"Yes, I was going this way when lightning struck me the first time."
Crushed. Pick at that scar until it ruptures—a new mouth to feed.

Shattered glass, according to our religion, but from this view, bodies.
Stare up—yes, this is the terrific sky, you are here, it's

heaven: bound for a thousand years this essence must be loosed
a little season, do not ask why, "while her spirit soars

her body struggles to live" from safe & selfishness. coldness. a poser
or pretender no more, but genuine gasp on a slashed throat, who

envies a shape pared down to survival its blood transfusion.
And having escaped, the woman on TV news sucks it like a kitten, you

shake, mouth, "That I was born for something in particular? silver scalpels cutting it apart,
& here I am with the usual worthless tune stuck in my craw and wasted day.

how many. children starving." but what looks like a sliding door of shining corrugated metal
collapse & all that is, stars, their fleet chromospheres, fall

I come quickly. Who loves & makes, let them love, let them take
this water of life freely. Surely I come quickly.

Chinese quake lake still rising
Nothing can stop you from following your fate.

Man slain by snake in paradise!

I was very upset after reading your article. (Notes, always only notes.) A good medicine
can have risks such as death, sorry. She came back and said, I think it's a sin,

it's weird it's very flattering, told mourners, "This was a man." Yessir. They found
his battered boat and paddle; meanwhile, he showed up at her door sounding

dirty and disheveled, with plans to open an ecoretreat. A lethal cocktail of methadone
& antidepressants, also five other drugs, the former Dancing with the Stars contestant

now former everything. Please don't inform the part of the brain that controls
a combination of exhaustion & stress, she goes deer hunting with a lover then dons

a pink wig without her headlights on. I'm happy to say I've bounced back from
my alleged suicide attempt. You really want to be with somebody, but next morning

you'll barely recall me, announce her furious boys in a joint statement. On day three, he asked
wax or real? Before that they'd kissed and caressed each other's backs

like good automatons with matching motorcycles & breast implants, they resembled
an ordinary, loving couple trying not to make idiots of themselves said witnesses.

Absolutely don't take the kids. The correct term for someone not actively serving is
former human, feels absolutely right. After mattress shopping who doesn't swim in ditches?

Finally, I need to say, thanks for the bikini-photo blog post, I needed every nipple. How
could you continue to let us believe our dad had died when / doesn't matter: this starry now!

Twelve million bees let loose as lorry overturns in Canada
Amathomancy. By the arrangement of dust.

A strange phenomenon, witnessed by Mr. Stone

Clearly light at the moment—(though in a day I may not be here. anything of
mystic sea / magic sky / of talk to me—) 3:15 in the afternoon.

Descried over Empress, Georgia, by a man hunting deer—"I like to
shoot 'em—got to rack 'em every year." (sirens cycling closer—dream they

don't come) I'm afraid I'll be left behind, I know I'll be left behind, but
please be patient, note feel, speed, color—I don't know what to do about it in

eight minutes say good-bye to this first / paradise—at the last second.
I hope it comes in my lifetime, but not yet, I need to get ready, I haven't

burning (too good to be true—near orbital limit now—glare's really thin, halo's
pale as a victim, moon eaten up along city streets, and soon / but you know where

we are & what we need, god, your grid color-coded / anxiously expecting his return.
That conflagration unable to be put out, over us unable to be saved.

Public spectrum to be auctioned
Iridescent. False promise, worthless (like a spangled garment).

Mystery of the pregnant man

For at least eighty minutes in Magnolia, Mississippi I sat curled inside my
dead mother as she lay on the kitchen floor. She'd been chopping onions.

Dear world, you leave us such strange clues to draw conclusions from: a rudimentary
beating heart, mad sack of face, nine perfect toes on one cleft foot. But how should we

bury this—blew a tooth out of his nose, & to our surprise & horror, someone's inside
this man who comes complaining of a stomach pain. But not someone: we tried

to ask or name it, but its one eye wouldn't blink, so we stowed it, no cure,
in formaldehyde for our new museum. Flourish of flesh, cellular smile—a bone spur,

we told him. But late nights, it whispers to me, "With this instrument, I see right through
your dull ordinary. Three thumbs are better than two, love is stronger than hate, inside you,

abnormal growth started at the age of ten, following a grave dream. He is still growing,
entirely rotten & hollow inside, the glittering cyst contains a primitive mind

that tells you what to do, but it doesn't matter: who is without a flaw?
You know life can be different than it is—the world is good & filled

with good people & most of them doing good deeds why then should we not
all smile & be happy?" Persistent infection in her brain. Shut down by the Humane Society

Smashed diamond
You're feeling like a slightly heightened version of yourself.

51

It's leukemia

Each spot each sample each symptom—that is why they call it a symptom, it
"has never stirred since an appendectomy when she was six, August 1941, Chicago"

—it points. In our special universe each shard of bone adds up, even the numbers
of the letters calculable, so fold them to learn why, finding and feeling a stronger

"still growing during his final illness" tendency to dust. stars above, aging, shedding, as a
landmine sheds] such a war, & you saved sometimes religious, sometimes ashes.

You'll bury, like a tree, in a coffin ten by nine. Sometimes stumbles—sometimes falls" to lie
under the sky flattens, listen, see flash flood in rapid lightning, fires, roar of thunder,

no wonder you hope for tongues, await forking, a touch, if he can touch
down in seven states causing millions in damage he can sure touch you.

Catch that comet whirling, when science comes to save you, you'll stay witnessing "that big
big man can be heard six miles away when he shouts at the top of his voice"

Calling. Another American, still living, claims to have been born near Washington, DC
in 1853, daughter of a freed slave, but no records are available to prove . . .

Girl, 16, survives lightning strike, family wins lottery the next day
Headphones. A message is conveyed to the wearer alone.

Debriefing the survivors

Want to ask you a question, show you my face. Want to ask you to show a face a
"Don't be afraid to be human" face "but I think of myself as deeply faceted like a

hope topaz show me your don't be afraid to be" [surely I shall be holy when I'm only
dust] "We couldn't get nothing out, just ourselves, our house jet

& garnet, lintels eaves flashings falling, "I'll never
forget one death. Well they may make it, but some of them may not—

miracle our fatalities & injuries were that low ("praise plasma") heard
it creaking, making noise it shouldn't make, and then it just started falling

apart. I would start at the foundation: root gnawed through.
But relax. And if you're still here, smile. It means someone's looking out for you.

Look out: bridge on the move
It's a diamond in the rough.

Rambo v. Bambi

That's the only reason I'm even alive. Once that truck rolled over me, my
arm hanging off by a little skin, it said you're not walking away from this. Didn't

hurt to get run over, it hurt when I saw, but since then I've seen some real rough stuff—
dark turned to light with one click, light turned to ice, the rest of real time

crushed in a fist. Daddy built a hole, called it a bomb shelter. Because the bomb
oh baby am in fragments am a split shatter cells then atoms quarks rocketing

but if you could cut it out would you cut it out: hatchet anonymous murder movies
—crosswise just hacking up just peeling loose viscera from the fascia just

baby freeing bone of the shank meat freeing meat of the shank bone unwrenching
tendon ligament loose weightless free & less the fast-spiraled unknitting selves severing

whirling sprung electrons from a storm, nuclei cut their cut-through burst a cloudburst cold
as radiation: we rain. acid-of-you we-tisane you-concentrate us-juice you-oil us-ooze

all up in a we-bomb yes a sever, assuredly. —Not a mark on their bodies,
can't tell how. The footage has since reportedly been destroyed.

Great Satan sits down with Axis of Evil
Dream of a funeral and attend a wedding.

Dance dude

Once upon a time,
The crime.

What are you looking at? fury.
Fastenings come undone—lighthouse not lit—this hour a fake &

oil slicks our ocean, the community destroys its common interest ounce by ounce,
so you must cease to be afraid

of coyotes, desert sounds. I wish none of this had ever happened,
losing their damn minds, he put a handgun to my head, scared, held

a silver penknife to your throat, bled, but no one injured, police said
terrified. "I don't know how to prevent, I don't know

how many times I stabbed her & I don't know why I stabbed her," no something is
happening, no [sleep with cleavers] lord,

we're being robbed of something here"—
while pearly everlasting, the mortician's flower, smiles rotlessly back at you.

[like the smell] [hell
is a place where they bring you drinks"

Archways that fall apart as you pass through. You see, nothing
really is as good as it looks, leave the groceries on the counter, boy, I'm tired.

But still I don't know"—your sister's death
in her garage, causes scatter like crows at a stone.

You must read the annals of the anarchist—nothing else
does justice to this year

Man opens fire at church festival in California
Cactus. Need to keep others away for various reasons. Feeling old. Feeling odd.

55

The thing with claws

Listen: Titanic, Hindenburg, cash earthquakes in Pakistan.
"Michael knew he shouldn't bring his AK-47 to the 7-11"

incurable morass. I don't mean to be flip about yr sundering crevasse, I'm just
not there myself today, that helpless dross is what the unsaved always say thus

"You want someone to understand you but it's impossible"
broken glass: love, you will understand by eating like a good dog does. Eternal

essence of nothing, colossal empty stance, fallen escape route, his massive legs, his
"signature gunpowder drawings & related outdoor explosion events" art terrors, less

"she was thankful they had a life at all." Such messes we must pass by. Clear as in dream-lives
"shown an ornate shield," thirty chargers of gold, a thousand silver knives,

perhaps I should write about race instead of going to ballet class. A comet
does not need you, a ruby does not care, what is it you want to hear? "the secret"

"please tell me" "I've been trying to tell you" well you've failed. Still
you happen not to have fallen in. And you've got a good angel to advise,

but nothing's personal these days, just editorials. "To judge by her patter
this one's empty, no message for you, just a mirrored silver platter."

Attacked by a lioness: long life.
Look around: someone out there needs you.

Diary X

Woe-weed grows between rows of history books black in gnaw-mold.
[remainder fragmented] [buried alive] ["talking to people like you"] We are alive

at a very interesting time in history: Israel, USSR, Miss America
lies scratchers shadow toxin gash blasphemy insanity feverpit incendiaries chain link

but how will we recognize there is a message at all?"
But why feel for a wounded stranger: "how will we recognize

the truth which conceals that there is none—impossibly perched fortifications
on fairy-tale hills. In case of war this concealing work has real importance

mind-dry, brain-ticked. You always wondered
what would happen if you kept going [small acids inlaid] blood-borne diseases, & eases

a mindfuck into the narrow channel of a school-bus aisle.
Fire alarm, single file, we leap in white flashing light, toss history books aside—

and you think you're immune, sparrow, too pretty for the pit?
There is going to come a time when it retracts its web with everyone still caught in it.

Myanmar death toll said to reach 15,000
The answer is no, no, a thousand times no.

57

The troubles

Be careful going home tonight: protect
your family in a culture that's gone stark raving mad, craving for firepower, sawn-

off shotgun level at an intruder's chest, handgun unless you feel it's your last chance,
use an explosive amount of force & threats, if so you are asking for a home-invasion robbery.

But welcome it when it comes, this miracle: reclaim your place
on a one-way bus, admire the rising sidearm as its owner misreads your Love,

the person growing, being replaced by the disease. Her tumor eats first: face
on the bed smiling today but with ever less recognition so I despaired forgive me I prepared

to take her room. I changed the locks. Throw rocks
at that silence, deface a guidepost in a dark forest, scream & kick

under the avalanche to make a space to breathe, for today,
the knowing is deafening. Tired of it working out? This is the lamentation

wherewith they shall lament her, or something like it, make thee perpetual
desolations, or very nearly, sigh sigh, aftermath always present around us already

haven't visited the grave lately. When the door's just shut, will I
nightmare of no more. Last night I dreamed I saved you from fire, will I

Vast cracks appear in arctic ice
This is not a safe place.

Audubon Society Field Guide to Disaster

In the famous cyclorama,
Raze the wooden schoolhouse to build an explosion.

An earthquake destroys the man-made waterfall hewn by Romans . . . designed
by Romans, hewn by their slaves—captives from all corners of the known world,

people you'll see in hell are here,   [in the famous torture]
Please lie still   I'd like the police to shoot me, if they could"

O what have I done. Brother, we're not staying here no more. Pure abyss. But we
are on the line now with an eyewitness: most of the victims have been

(shadows breathe) (stars ache) (a universe) This is a very hard thing to watch.
Run through a burning building, gallows or courthouse, soon beams split asunder & iron

storm-mass crashes directly into our Pillar of Fire church. We expect the usual
mushroom cloud, so be especially suspicious / superstitious

among strangers, fast, sudden, and forcefully to the eyes, nose, or throat
"without concern for the damage you might inflict"

Illinois man changes name to "In God We Trust"
Grammar. Studying it indicates the dreamer is trying to do the right thing.

When the dust clears, we find you

who by intrepid conduct saved three children from a burning house at the
cost of her own young life: daughter of a bricklayer's laborer, April 24, 1885.

who lost his life in averting a serious accident to a lady whose horses were unmanageable,
saved six persons from fire, but in his last act scorched. Voluntarily

descended into a high-tension chamber to rescue two workmen overcome
by poison gas, drowned in attempting to save his brother after he himself

just rescued—Harry Sisley, age ten. (commemoration of heroic self-sacrifice) who
refusing to be deterred from making three attempts to climb a burning staircase to

save her aged mother, died of the effects, saved a lunatic woman from suicide at Woolwich
Arsenal Station but was himself run over by the train. Elizabeth Coghlan, age twenty-six

in saving her family and house by carrying blazing paraffin to the yard, crushed in trying
to save her sister from a steam engine, lost his footing reaching, risked poison

rather than lessen any chance of saving a child's life / and died. a carman,
friend on a desperate venture to save two girls from a quicksand themselves

engulfed. who was drowned near London Bridge. with Alice Maud Denham striving
to save her children from a burning house in Bethnal Green to save a companion

Nepal reborn as a republic
Fountain. Success comes from devotion.

Questions to ask your family doctor

But just a second: what part of this proves I'm alive? I incline to the opposite of
solipsism, i. e., the same thing, a me-shaped hole in the system

of ballgames & strippers with leather chaps & low-grade housing. Whatever the score, we
are not part of the report, are the left-out, average, unchanged, tranquil

reader. "There was a war on. I'd heard of GIs, but skimmed love poems, skipped news.
Now the bombing of a temple is a part of my courtship—Buddhas of Bamiyan—

still I never met a casualty." Afraid we're too complacent about politics, sure
no good will come of it anyway, I paid, voted, woke & was holding a gun—this one here,

smoking & empty, while everyone around phones home. Isn't true nothing
changes—my mother gets older, weeds grow, friends bury their darling

& the question remains: are you a force for good in the world?
"America is a force for good in the world." Body armor & bullets, missile shield

My paper reminds me to end. I deny nothing. What can one be sure of? Partake
of the family picnic. God knows where the meat comes from. Break the wonder bread.

Monkeys think, moving artificial arm as own
Adieu. Desire to be better educated.

Catatonia

Quiet. A single amount of the void spun around, split off, self-expanding into a
wormhole tachyon torus & absence of time as a substance in motion, for everything is

called into spin [dancer) (listen, dancer]: all prior philosophy forgot, useless, hence
Light extends a fine quality (cloth of gold, silver), invisible to the

Dark—"Before us spins a diamond covered in cloud—" (these were merely
roil we borrow from current flame, we borrow (vacant collections of potential

nothing from flame / priceless "shone then in the pitch" of your marrow, tomorrow, honey
I tried but the doctors said, they stamped, let her die, her T-cells / no transplant

flowers here like a pink atamasco lily. Too many peonies in my
mindlessness—asylum burning . . . all a profoundly meaningless | garden—given eye

For there is only one wisdom. In the presence of its finer rain, the larger solid particles
of longer wavelengths of energy | shatter, as though stones falling on us

Cyclone slams into main Myanmar city
Dead (person). An overwhelming fear of loss.

62

Blazon

We come closer to the heart of the mystery, salvaging or scavenging this autopsy of
home—rattles like shock treatment, crow feathers [from our other side] & no

yearling soul dances in these blood groves. Toward a more perfect, & so I slur,
"here, bequeath thee this portrait of myself, done in costly silks,

as I expect to appear upon rising, sometime happy bone-face & fascia,
stay, surely god recognizes my" atomized. More perfect mortality. Lack

torches us, "in flames, but so happy to be alive" while each reached eye
tries.—"Funny how you go rambling on when all's grave goods already." Hope? No, so neon

hotly shows how a shinbone outlives its skin, poor men: gilt & enamel coffins, in them
ourselves—sinking in the oubliette of our eyed head, dressed, yes, but ache

unaneled. Why? What's this flesh wish that its uttermost text dries silent white?

4,400-year-old mummy unearthed, smiling
Metoposcopy. From the lines of the forehead.

Aria of the metal detector

At the airport, brand-new people drag their luggage in pleathery uncertainty.
The world's capacity is exceeded, you are the excess.

On vast lounge TVs, brave explorers circumnavigate our globe until
"they killed our mirror, our light, & our one true guide"—perhaps not excess, blessed

exception. Alarms ring. So you want someone to understand you?
Severe pain or suffering, in order to create

orange alert. But you garble in a hundred ways your inborn message. Spectacular
dust—what are you going to do about it? something is wrong

while four elderly lesbians nibble at oatmeal raisin cookies, safe
& plastic as you will be elsewhere, but here, "I'm almost paralyzed, almost not able

to move—we're trivial right up until we prove eternal—mere
ganglia dangling like hacked-out wires, innards in a

oh well. Who can be suspended
like a pendulum over the matter/natter of a life. Who can't?

"I don't want to go, but at least I'll know." Light curves around each molten face,
a clerk asks for volunteers to quit this flight. You could travel inward,

given time. When & where should one resolve: but hear the flourish
as our universe begins over again. What wish? Turns out your groan's middle merely, filler.

Unexceptional events set off fatal blaze
Aleuromancy. By means of flour.

Dull as a mile

This day breaks hazy, ready with thunders & corresponding sorrows / sparrows.
This encounter persists, a series of fruitful misprisions of yours & mine. Minerals.

"And when I had heard & seen, I fell down to worship" warships.
You must forgive the scar, for your body with its unmending hurts / hawks

may represent an unexpected message, mission—you are gifted
with a natural intuition—use it: unnatural intervention—choose it: "I myself

have made a difference—have wrought catastrophe, monotony" money,
tattering, & rip an ancient text open to the sufferings of modern men & women

your urinary tract infection, your losing bet. "The span kept collapsing, down down down
until it got to me" "we saw cars plunge off, people in the water" waver "you'll never

cross a bridge again without thinking of this"

Amazon Indians attack official over dam project
You have not waited too long.

What the thunder said

As you are greeting this new fate cycle, note the many eyes staring at you. Explore
what might be happening: if a worm crawls on your mother, it measures her

for a dream. Examine news: examine what needs to happen: listen to news
with open jaws. The bees will leave unless, when a mockingbird sings at night, if a hen crows

but mostly a man's shroud resembles a suit of clothes, left open at the back. Understand
just how visible you are, don't let others decide when dogs howl, the world

hears what you say right now. If a bird flies into your house, by no means beat
at it with a broom but turn the mirror to the wall. Aim for more of what you want,

less lightning. Some people claim if you touch, act as though you feel power, when
a grave sinks early it's a sign another will follow soon. Think, trace, lead, listen.

"The foundation has already been laid"
Christ. Very important message, whatever it is.

Can this last long?

Look—and glean the nothing from the scene. Sight remains your most helpless
sense, admits a world with no use for you. No, you shut up. "And the first

foundation, jasper" shift us leftward, we need our "just got back
from Iraq" second layer of storm. Shut out. In the midst of this utter crap, a letter:

"Was it a play or something?" you will query the stage: 10,000 Somalis
can't be, you'd like to be depressed but you've taken too much St.-John's-wort—

morbid, baby, more bored, save me, bound for more moribund daily flights to
pandemonium—"wish I had less me" "hate me, do you too?" "wish I was a rose of

explosion, rattling with odors, a sickle & a skeleton key—and riches, wisdom, strength,
honor, glory, blessing, and a teenage girl huddled under the overpass.

In other news, your sick little brother sent me to ask, in heaven, will I still be sad
for the unsaved in my family? What's it really like up there—paths of gold,

what kind of gold? My mom & I think white gold. Blind & her daughter
paraplegic and she / people disappear, things blow up / I am sure

as I stand here of God's love for you. I loved a dead pet in the same way. We are
salespeople for the good news so try it on. Now let's listen as Mr. Leon defines rapture.

Into the dirt
You're just the person to make something glorious of the dross.

67

But can you care about the wide world living all your life in Monticello, Florida?
True, he did bomb occupied cities once, he does know things:

"I saw they scream like men, their homes burn like ours—
so leave me alone—I've got okra to plant."

Yes, you've got a lovely garden here. What do you put in the soil?
"Nothing that isn't already there." Tell us more?

"It's all still there. I hear on the other side we'll meet again, in an orchard.
But not yet. Weed, and wait for the glitch in the hour to be repaired.

Take my neighbor—longs to know what part of Africa he's from.
What if you trace yourself to one coffin ship & find—sin of those diagrams—I don't

want to die a complete negative in life, you think it is a secret
shut like a moth in a night flower, you think it will stay quiet—

signature that guards the compass star that steers the vessel & her cargo
a contrary tug of tide & million fish that hurtle sleek & scaled & free the other

way: a relative of yours once had his say on human frames, tightest way to pack them
in a middle passage, while he sleeps safe harbor. Quietly all's unhinged until we

Recognize yourself: living on acres of voice. When you spoke to me, then / echo I
could not help but understand it after a while. garden refurbished & ready"

Belshazzar's

       "That translation | means nothing. My original / these pauses
have infected / —all cells \ by this time— / only foals on a nightfall hillside / —only

spores / reaching towards— | nor can it be said "To know [you feel it because I say you will] is to receive is
                                           chrysoprase

underflow [inner] this storm has any heart or soul   third world
invulnerable . . . dancer pirouettes along a razor edge   . . . However,

a natural disaster is being made   anoint it
into a man-made catastrophe   lament it]

& misfortune. _____. "I know this way to its very end I have traversed
this bottomless breath until it extinguished all light and joy"

—enough to feed 100,000 people for eight days. Runaways get away
through night like constellations of the Southern Hemisphere" Safe house cold as

"nor can it be said a story
 has any universal or objective meaning"

Man declared dead "feels pretty good"
Today is the first day of the way back.

69

You don't think so

I'm the one who's always right: the Author. Now I'll burn you; you'll feel little bites.
Then I thought for the first time people might be dead—a huge thunder & metal on

(ouch) (fragments) in the bathroom of a home
found unharmed in a home on a tree-lined street, in the walled garden of an unharmed

which is history written in advance. Babe, I wanted to save you but I wasn't sure
those were real rocks they were flinging. "Stop having problems!" Darling, I'd prefer

to be less difficult, but fastened to this world of intense & excruciating pain,
Charlton Heston ceased today. Do you think that's right, god? Explain!

But you can help no one by trying. On the contrary, you must try.
This dream does not lend itself to explication. It's personal, it's all personal,

but some persons are more valid than others. ("unsaved
don't know the difference between right & wrong") Still,

even a criminal's house is brightly lit on Christmas Eve
baby, even a maniac loves his mother. "he may pass them by as meaningless

"meaningless words, invented merely
*

—you'll have to forgive the silences. I meant it all kindly, not as a false trail
that leads I am afraid directly to the jaws of the lion.

Army buried study faulting Iraq planning
Ace. One needs top-notch help.

70

Such rich hour

I tell you true, this day you will be with me in paradise. So
here are your lift tickets, your goggles to guard against snow blindness, for the sky's

bright beyond novae. Good-bye to the body, feather-fine, brittle bone & smile—
for the living know that they will die, but the dead know nothing.

No, nothing. And you can call & call & listen to his recorded voice—
visit him on YouFace & see his last, now stateless status—but nothing" nothing"

oh well. Still, say when you go, you travel like a space probe, alone & out to perihelion—
or, in the grave, under earth, open your mouth—white betony root burrows into

your (used to be) sense—sight a worm crawling distantly, feel a skinless chill,
and what you taste—circulation of rivers across this vast continent at last?

We can hope, can't we. Our mortal bodies dirt-hidden, but
our eternal souls—details. Don't let it end this way, tell them I said something. I said

I can listen with all my heart but can I utter it so we understand? Nothing
good enough, significant enough to end with. Death is,

in this learned man's opinion, at least sometimes bad for those who die. But why?
No one is there to feel it. No one can say she has ceased & is dismayed.

Dreaming on
Crux: will receive wishes.

71

Trying real hard now

Ultimately, it was god who decided. We will not have anything to complain about or be
saddened by / Here gleams (forever)

platinum paving, a pavé diamond overpass. There is no procreation or loneliness.
"He's got morals, principles. He is remembered chiefly for his roles

as Michelangelo, Moses & Ben-Hur. Later in life he led the National Rifle
unexplained presence of things"

like dog leashes, choke collars, & bungee cords. Brood first
on the kind of ideas a disaster unleashes: "this day

the bridge fell, for no reason, I drove past. I had a feeling" a burning bush
hisses, arm thyself, "Fasten your doors; at midnight,

home invasion. Man shot / girlfriend cries, "he was only
no death, no anger, mirror. And in ochre trace with one finger immortal lineaments.

Follow the silt
A picture falling: look elsewhere.

Central heat

That arm extended raveling clockwise, a balance spar—something
grows out of nothing. Hate a center, depart from a center, abandon

an empty center: "it violates our private space & the one place
we think of as our sanctuary." Lift your animal head, drink of

always this unfastening: our wish clears out, leaving space for heaven, but not
heaven, we were there once, naming, clawing ourselves—an element like arrows

or rainwater shatters off your arm, fractured, not cut diamond, is star sapphire
built around a flaw. Some home invaders might have walked

in your house before—saw themselves in your mirrors. Some even claim "it's a
rush"—that hush before you hurt or save, suddenly sure of where you stand.

Kansas wheat harvest finally under way
Dream of tears is consolation.

Take the long way home

The child sets out in a canoe, arm-paddling; the boat becomes, at a distance to us, limbed.
To me your life is news. (Mystery just how this works.)

Once, on the way there,
a flock of wild turkeys appeared along the road, walking stately, in order.

Was I asleep an hour ago? Loving you
is the great episode—came to you in your sleep in the summer garden, poured in your ear a

yes—oh, and I'm still wearing your ring" shifts,
arms in a silk fire, casting shadow & line, sinker, "gets colder

every day" up to your waist beside the dock, lower half erased as a moon is. Flashing
fleshes illustrate nerve movement of a thought. Hook. She's almost to the spit. Sun—and is

gone, passes away like a glint off fish scales, generous
wave repeating each gentle difference—and you were going to say?

All we are waiting for is" "world hasn't ended yet"   "every single thing
you love could be gone in a flash"   [paradise inside you]

Alive. Watch her dangling, stringing instants, nestling one in another—she turns—
you turn and a [eagle shadow] pupil her continual grid of focus, follow, trim mind follows, the

"soul" / electrons exit enter no hello, good-bye. Watch the girl—cell death as hand shifts eye
finds heart birth as hand rises to finger out the only galaxy visible to the naked eye. Fly by—

these birds know nearly everything about air currents, your future
so trust yourself to thermals, gliding smoothly over Ararat

Minnehaha Falls' walls are falling
Gull. Bridge between the worlds of sleeping and waking. If flying, freedom.

Treasure of the Sierra Madre

Be careful when visiting this lovely place: a falls can change your life.
The unknown kills you—a landslide's clarification of your relation to the garden.

Look here, where we see the merely bodily resemblance fade—
world's wonder turns to ash in hissing air, thusly a convict & his lovely

jihad push through flashbulb galaxies until erased, cyst, embryo wholly effaced, yes,
we all rush along an inside rib to reach the reason for the season of dust, yes,

always a listener's burden to let groans be themselves, never more
man-made theories or emission of human emotion rather than sentiments

than moans. Always a listener's groan. That expressway of sighs—"
broke off. Vehicles that quaver, laden, that collapse. That sentiments. That despair—

Why? was not I my face, my hands" moans home among roses, man-made
garden, machined Eden, closed Mondays but millionaire in precious moss

they gave after their ability unto the treasure of the work.
And descended, like dark into / hearts of flame   —

But that is beautiful—where did it come from?
The nature of light is not suited to explanation.

Mind over mountain
Thread a needle three times and tie it around your neck at night; in the morning, the pain will be over.

75

St. Catherine

Then this happened. He would walk but overrun by a tank's tread / bent
bone cradled over the nutmeat of a memory: drain & hair caught in his fingers

possibly dead fingers. Beyond this fence, thousands, friends, a great sifting is
being done. What you obey, weighed. And now a pause while a man in shades

"roughs someone up" / Angels. See with a blind child's eyes: the great physician
signs a death certificate, sweet body wracked, what you took for a voice

rattles. Sometimes I get so frightened as I read. The power becomes the power
& we & all other partial mechanisms teeter to its flow on this transient machine: crows

need to be fed, rain of salt. Don't confess the effect of these shock lights, a wrist
lame in them, your own of course. Don't break, pray, say, "I am doing a short work of great
                                                            witnessing—"

A guided tour of your body
Box. Long journey. Death. Womb.

Paradise

There: between sea and land, four hold a fifth among them—moonlit, flashing shadow.
How do they move—toward earth or ocean? Must be a rescue—he touched a depth

empty of air, a pure blue fear, but strong hands saved him & brace him while the sea
releases, breath returning to each niche of his lungs—that's the shaking you see. Or is it

ecstasy—almost free, now he writhes while the others struggle to bind these lashing octopi
in the shape of a man, hoping to make him speak, be their brother again. Or do you witness

(silently, voiceless) a drowning: like pallbearers they hold him level, face to the moon,
showing him for a last gasp the mortal view that he, innocent or guilty, knows no

ultimate word can save, the wave in their eyes surviving him—and does he cry out,
flying close to his horizon, or treasure what will inundate him limb by limb as its cool verge

forever stirs toward an end he clearly sees, but you don't see it, only this scene you scan
eagerly as Daddy drives by, drives home, the road drones but a glimpse is enough to seed

riddles in a hundred years of dreams (you live that long), codes of all slipping loose, dull
iris blossoms again ink-blue, no one can have your life back from the foam, or will he

never remember this—moment half-free half-forced, branches of his mind, roots of his
groundless nerves filling with liquid will while the exorcism plies above him, burns above us.

His job: magician
In some area of your life, you are just arriving.

The last words of Alex, the African gray parrot

I haven't had champagne in a long time. Home to the palace to die.
I am content, I am confused, either expression is correct. Pardon me,

sir, I did not do it on purpose. Codeine & bourbon, we got a bad fire,
why hast thou. Fear nothing. It's very beautiful over there, beautiful, all lost: empire,

body, & soul. You be good, see you tomorrow, I love you. "Don't leave me": No.
We are holding our own, we must be on you but cannot see you,

this is the last of earth, the earth is suffocating. So here it is, what is it? Can't
you stop this? I can't sleep—little cousins, called back. It's stopped. I want

nothing but death. Get the sledge ready, I want to go see my sister. Please don't let me fall.
Why not / so hard to / kaput. I really need a therapist. I have not told half of what I saw.

Hurricane's eye passes calmly over town
Diamond. A very positive symbol of endurance, purity, and invulnerability.

Ms. Truth

Do you know what I've seen? until the flesh was deeply lacerated & blood streamed—
his back twisted like these fingers of mine, like roots of a tree.

Let me understand it for myself. I have ears to hear, a mind to understand.
"A kind master to his slaves" "slaves, horses, and other cattle" "for the sum of one hundred

dollars" "cellar assigned to his slaves" "too old to be sold" "dismal chamber" "gentle to his slaves" But I make
no comment on facts like these, I believe

the Lord is as close as he can be, and not be it.
("I would've put my tomahawk in his head") ("Oh no missus no")

Like the rest of you, I have come here to hear what I have to say.
A young woman of fine appearance and high standing in society, the pride of her husband,

was beating in the skull of a slave-woman named Tabby.
Those stars are the same stars, these the same trees. I am not going away—I'll

stay here and stand the fire. [all bruises & putrefying sores]
Again that voice: I know you, and I don't know you. I know you; who are you?

Now the war begins. (Tabby murdered & buried in the garden.)
I took a new name—it was never so light before, it was too much light."

C'est la vie. Suddenly Sojourner on the bone of the earth
traveling a ragged foot: and suddenly ceases, midst of her saying.

Baghdad wakes up to rare snowfall
Eromancy. By exposing objects to the air.

Voyager

This is a present from an infant, distant world: we are trying
to survive our time so we may live into yours.

What's this?—one weighs, listens to the box.
You can race sunset all day long if you fly west fast enough—eternal life, only

"clover over another lover of yours": the no one rooms.
I see no way out. "then some cataclysm"—thousands of years of rain

create our ocean, blank as a stone fist at first but soon teeming
with motion, onward mumbling faces, seeing the force before it comes

it comes. I was alone once, it was terrifying.
We travel across a blue waste between stars . . .

Nothing else happens, the apparition never named, its omen unfallen, but still they hold
that prayer at arm's distance, saying, I feel it is important because it's true.

What's this? As long as it lasts it ends. Terminal, you'll murmur, "Doctor,
I see myself dancing. I know it's not real, but I still see it."

Death blow
Exhale. Not worried about anything anymore.

PARADISIACAL

(the dream of William Bartram)

[The girl you almost were speaks. Gradually,
in chorus, rise out of dark to crescendo,
then break off to listen to her.]

We enter the wilderness.

Remember this? The way
a pine stand at the top of a hill combs light

that is equatorial platinum here, turning
needles colorless glass at closer glance.

Tunneling through (I think this will destroy you)

Your wound mirror   stare into our void center, here among

Imagine   sudden dawns, hurtles in on us   Is Desire   cut through cataracts could

Drown—kiss inside your wrist kisses back flickering arrowing their endless

Aquifer pure as dirt, throat raw from singing, turning

Your animal head side to side, stepping from one bone to another like stones in a clear pool, your

Own spine like a pine tree in a tornado, only you were the wind—summoned for your form

Of a storm, swift good-bye that was in your breathless "overtakelessness"

"When we were young and it rained like this,
 we'd put our swimsuits on and go out in the yard
                                        and swim in the air"

83

We explore a vast plain, lake bed, or swamp.

. . .

clover honey we find in a beaten tree nothing is made of its make nothing of its

. . .

—almost endless green plain & meadows—
—there alone all night, look

. . .

up through orb weavers' webs while white lichen bark-spots make a line in the mind

. . .

They have hollowed the trunks with their singing

. . .

                                                          saying at the same time, You are come, can
You live in a quarter turn, pane of glass, a midstep misstep—burn between a mockingbird's notes—

. . .

we took our rest there under the shade of   Wandering

. . .

sedge's thousand rustling stems, am of matter, unsoul, lakelike, fed & ebbing   :   wavescape

. . .

veiled or drowned—suddenly lightless—in wings now—swarmed   "my first memory," she
                                                              murmurs—a field, her daddy (unfinished

. . .

. . .

solace that stretches a long ways into the marsh, mist invisible made visible More

. . .

Mysteries: these listening in love   was we ocean wild   & wet to the heart

. . .

while here, other little hands unfolding, first red then viridian—
wild geranium.   Birdnoise all the time now)

. . .

84

[*With great desire, walking around
the light in the center.*]

Who will you love now that the arrow has left you
with more room in your heart?

❉

Dear limbo, dear star of crushing gravity,

❉

this road runs into the sea: good-bye, despair
where's wreck. what's under drives. you'd

live in a tumbledown house if you could"

❉

Most feeling ghost,

❉

I felt only that no coast was enough
—miles only you see have seen will see must save. saint

We hurt for the entrance or hunted it

❉

Dear avalanche, dear vertebral rhyme,

❉

You never saw a star like here. you heard
a seeing being, burning
in the turning toward

Your nature: storm center. Enter

this chrysalis, so lightly shed, & step
free like the latent half

afterlife in these sloughs. Lantern, I love
the way you aren't where you go"

❉

85

[Abandon unison and speak at will. Choose,
whisper, listen. The last voice belongs
to the one you've always loved.]

We come upon ruins in the forest.

(remember this from the dream you always forget:

stars for doors
walls of wet passion vine)

Dear, you

disrobe before a mirror in a distant motel,   Let all see

Longingly
Cerulean
Celadon

elixir
root
messenger

Undress
Say my name
Empire(less)

Brush fire, I

follow your horse scent over miles
abandoned, or Undone
shore (moves by desire)
of a soul, unearthed or earthing
fields of this endless, & yes
breathe on the haint glass, last
midnight's room
was loved once
when in mossy distance
among crowds, the whirlwind
Shh: lawless

[*Listening, chanting. Let a crown
rise from your head.*]

Now ceilings give way in algal bloom:

take up your lodging on the border of an ancient burial ground,

And hid in cypress, embrace of vetch—acre of rapture

& build fields of solid satin, & hang what's left of death on a wall

Also a single vase full of earth to remind us we are

Sojourner

Still under, asunder

but lovely self, inviolate

Shall spin, spun gold

Luminaria

(yes I did learn the name)   we like all others

bankrupt, treasure, touching

her ruin, murmur "this plant is sensate, not dead wood"

So we came closer

& free in this great house's ash, our other

House: of shadow but shadow

made weight of light & free in the dream we

Burn our chains & they burn, blaze lynch

live oak rises till roots trail over the land & in its roots

will grow lymph, fat, bone will

resurrection fern

I know you now

87

[*Talking again to each other. Lie down
where you like: even if the water
covers you, you will be seen.*]

We enter the water.

And I came upon a vast sink where people were living,
climbing out of the hollows, souls in their hands,
(how a glyph can shift its stone),

Lost
ghost of a self   Leaf-self

above & below me, suddenly, ocean. gaze for miles. smooth shapes wing their way out—manta & lightning

cannot be harnessed   mulberry at the corner. Hillside of horse mint buzzing"
& that wheat field in wind on your arm

—
This longing space. Came close   In lover or shudder
                                                   Lichen on your face: found

                              (. . . wanderers like ourselves, dressed in their own hides and
                                                    heads aquiver in fallen feathers
—You are closer than ever to being water—

Always the same sheer
how did we come here   (covering, un-

sleeper more beautiful. kiss unscarring, halo unheld,

—
How will you course the wave of your wish?   sea-green seething around you here

                                                      you want to
                                                      hurt be hurt how

Seaweed eats through a pier as your wrist through steel—all raw tendon & this
pleasure in cutting
loose: arose

veil : live

free : reel

force : voice

whispering : grasspools

We lose our way.

That it should be more & How

Let go your

star. Ocean opening her deadly
above that thread of
ease love
so easy

If you are a galaxy

Seared by your flight—
arrow in the blood

(call it a wound but it shines)

The Eveningstar Rain Lily, *Cooperia drummondii,* opens in the evening, stays open for a day or two, and emits delightful perfumes. Like some other warm-climate plants, it is pollinated by night-flying creatures. It is the most luminous of flowers, standing out in the moonlight. It also faces absolutely upward, in a plane perpendicular to the stem.

The species was discovered in the 1830s, growing in Texas. My plants were rescued from the site of the downtown public library when construction was commencing. I talked a workman into digging up the clump of leaves (not knowing exactly what the plant was), and we split them. I hope he has enjoyed his as much as I enjoy mine.

The plants are not large—about the size of the rest of the rain lilies. They do appear after a good rain, yet, for some reason, sprinklers don't seem to bring them out as well.

In this photo it emits a ghostly glow—the color seems to be too much for the camera to handle!

Taken from the center & thus we see what held there all
along,

:

—as if carried offstage mid-leap &

turns an arch: storm roaring through the

land, "I was raised by wolves Love

we runaways, we strays

& I will lose myself in oleander, I will lose

whose cold skin burns the glass, wave tears the shore,

shore harnessing the wave for
her own destruction:

The waste space saw & Loved you

Sources and Notes

Quotation marks do not always indicate quotation. Any voice might be familiar or a stranger. Orphaned punctuation is intentional. What closes and has not opened or opens without closing—interruption, weather, the ongoing. Understories may leave a mark or sink. As instructed in "Hanging gardens," sometimes you might look down, or across, for a way out.

TREASURE

Once, in a museum, I came across a vase as tall as me, twice as wide around as I could reach, priceless, ornate, in pristine condition, and absolutely hideous. I was fascinated: I had never seen such a concrete representation of the cruelty of unequally distributed resources. For this thing to exist and survive, for someone to have the surplus necessary to commission and preserve such a worthless ornament, someone else (probably many someones) had to be deprived, had to suffer.

On the other hand, I was also reading up on kabbala around the same time. I love how, in this system of reading and interpreting, a text is encrusted with love and labor until it actually begins to mean more than it first did. I love the idea of attention soaking into its object, altering, enriching it. I find something similar in the best of fashion—fantastic skins that armor and reveal, celebrate and distort.

Spurred by these influences, I began to think of a writing that might aim at total decadence and revelation at the same time, that might be prodigal in every sense.

This, then, is more an exploration of methods and materials of a potential hell than a tour of an actual hell. A paradise might be built the same way.

Sources include *A Journal of the Plague Year* by Daniel Defoe (Penguin Classics, 1966); *Jewelry* by Clare Phillips (Thames & Hudson, 1996); *Mourning Dress* by Lou Taylor (Routledge, 2009); *A History of Make-Up* by Maggie Angeloglou (Littlehampton Book Services, 1970); *The Cathedrals' Crusade* by Ian Dunlop (Taplinger, 1982); and *Vogue* magazine.

ZODIAC

Fascinated with tarot's limited system of iconic situations, I came up with a twenty-word zodiac I meant to represent all possible experiences. The zodiac rapidly fell apart, but the idea of a limited text that might convey all meanings remained—and led me to think about how people read. I've already mentioned kabbala;

Christian fundamentalism and Gnosticism also became important here, as well as daily horoscopes and disaster news. I thought about reading as if your life depends on it, reading a covert text, reading a text that is entirely about you, reading and trying to feel for strangers through the thin medium of words.

"Stillwater" is for Jay.

"Mystery of the pregnant man" is indebted to various sites on "freaks." The pregnant man lived in India. The freak show was shut down by the Humane Society. The final wish for a better world belongs to Medusa Van Allen.

"Dance dude" is for and from Carl Flink.

"Diary X" and "Catatonia" borrow from the writings of Jonathan Barlow Gee. Thank you, Jon, for your generosity, and, as you say, PEACE.

"When the dust clears, we find you": the Commemoration of Heroic Self-Sacrifice can still be seen in London's Postman's Park. Plaques were created beginning in 1900; in 2009 a new plaque was added, the first in more than seventy years.

"Questions to ask your family doctor" is for Jay, again. Also for Paul and Jennifer's Isabel.

"Blazon": John Donne wanted a painting of himself as he expected to look upon rising from the grave.

"Aria of the metal detector": Some words belong to my cousin Aaron Thomas Johnson (1971–2010).

"Central heat" is for Lise Houlton, Melanie Verna, Sarah Fox, and others.

"Paradise" takes its central image from a poem by Franck André Jamme.

"Ms. Truth" contains quotations from *The Autobiography of Sojourner Truth* (originally 1850; http://digital .library.upenn.edu/women/truth/1850/1850.html).

"Voyager" is for my grandmother, Edith Duncan Johnson (1913–2010).

Other sources include *Gödel, Escher, Bach* by Douglas Hofstadter (Basic Books, 1999); *Words* by Paul Dickson (Dell, 1983); *The Gnostic Gospels* by Elaine Pagels (Vintage, 1989); *Buying the Wind* by Richard M. Dorson (University of Chicago Press, 1964); *The New American Dream Dictionary* by Joan Seaman and Tom Philbin (NAL Trade, 2006); 1984 *Guinness Book of World Records* edited by Norris McWhirter and Ross McWhirter (Bantam, 1984); phrontistery.info; the *Minneapolis Star-Tribune;* the *New York Times;* Google news; Wikipedia; and *People* magazine.

PARADISIACAL

William Bartram (1739–1823) was an early American naturalist. His *Travels* of 1791 (Peregrine Smith, 1980) records journeys in the Southeast, especially Florida, from 1774 to 1776. The book was a great success, especially in England, where his description of Blue Springs inspired Coleridge in his description of the fountain in "Kubla Khan." Some of my ancestors were living in Florida by the time of Bartram's journeys; others arrived in the years after.

Chris Schlichting's *love things* inspired me with the idea of pure gratification. Great thanks to Alison Morse's Talking Image Connection reading series, where this form was first tested. Movement inspiration and other formal ideas come from many Twin Cities dancers and choreographers.

"Paradisiacal" is for the gardeners and the botanists, especially my mother, Melanie Johnson Darst.

"overtakelessness" is from M. C. Hyland.

"The Eveningstar Rain Lily," et cetera, is from Melanie Darst's bulb-a-week email.

❖

THANKS

Thanks to the publications and editors who published poems from this manuscript, sometimes under different titles: *Diagram* (Ander Monson), the *Antioch Review* (Judith Hall), *Volt* (Gillian Conoley), *Shoot the Moon* (Jonathan Thomas), *Spork* (Jamison Crabtree), *Triquarterly Online* (Dana Norris and Beth Herbert), *Typo* (Adam Clay and Matthew Henriksen), *Paper Darts* (Meghan Murphy, Jamie Millard, and Courtney Algeo), *Whole Beast Rag* (Katharine Hargreaves and Grace Littlefield), *trnsfr* (Alban Fischer), and *Black Warrior Review* (Dara Ewing).

Thanks to everyone who shared texts and ideas with me, including countless dancers and choreographers, whose names would fill another book; the Front Sparrows; other poetry compatriots and coconspirators across the country; and, as always, Corinne Duchesne. Great thanks go to everyone at Coffee House: Linda for sudden color, Anitra for indefatigably editing my monster, Kelsey, Caroline, Allan, Anna, Sarah, and the Board. Special thanks to Erika for late-night brilliance and champagne opera. And thanks to Chris for the yes.

Finally, thanks to my family for the mystery.

Colophon

DANCE was designed at Coffee House Press,
in the historic Grain Belt Brewery's Bottling House
near downtown Minneapolis.
The text is set in Caslon.

COFFEE HOUSE PRESS

The mission of Coffee House Press is to publish exciting, vital, and enduring authors of our time; to delight and inspire readers; to contribute to the cultural life of our community; and to enrich our literary heritage. By building on the best traditions of publishing and the book arts, we produce books that celebrate imagination, innovation in the craft of writing, and the many authentic voices of the American experience.

Funder Acknowledgment

Coffee House Press is an independent, nonprofit literary publisher. Our books are made possible through the generous support of grants and gifts from many foundations, corporate giving programs, state and federal support, and through donations from individuals who believe in the transformational power of literature. Coffee House Press receives major operating support from Amazon, the Bush Foundation, the McKnight Foundation, from Target, and in part from a grant provided by the Minnesota State Arts Board through an appropriation by the Minnesota State Legislature from the State's general fund and its arts and cultural heritage fund with money from the vote of the people of Minnesota on November 4, 2008, and a grant from the Wells Fargo Foundation of Minnesota. Support for this title was received from the National Endowment for the Arts, a federal agency, and through special project support from the Jerome Foundation. Coffee House also receives support from: several anonymous donors; Suzanne Allen; Elmer L. and Eleanor J. Andersen Foundation; Around Town Agency; Patricia Beithon; Bill Berkson; the E. Thomas Binger and Rebecca Rand Fund of the Minneapolis Foundation; the Patrick and Aimee Butler Family Foundation; the Buuck Family Foundation, Ruth Dayton; Dorsey & Whitney, LLP; Mary Ebert and Paul Stembler; Chris Fischbach and Katie Dublinski; Fredrikson & Byron, P.A.; Sally French; Anselm Hollo and Jane Dalrymple-Hollo; Jeffrey Hom; Carl and Heidi Horsch; Alex and Ada Katz; Stephen and Isabel Keating; Kenneth Kahn; the Kenneth Koch Literary Estate; Kathy and Dean Koutsky; the Lenfestey Family Foundation; Carol and Aaron Mack; Mary McDermid; Sjur Midness and Briar Andresen; the Nash Foundation; the Rehael Fund of the Minneapolis Foundation; Schwegman, Lundberg & Woessner, P.A.; Kiki Smith; Jeffrey Sugerman and Sarah Schultz; Patricia Tilton; the Archie D. & Bertha H. Walker Foundation; Stu Wilson and Mel Barker; the Woessner Freeman Family Foundation; Margaret and Angus Wurtele; and many other generous individual donors.